bill bissett

ANANSI

Othr buks by bill bissett

where is miss florence riddle (luv); we sleep inside each othr all (ganglia); (Th) Gossamer Bed Pan; Sunday Work (?); liberating skies; lost angel mining co.; what poetiks; s th story i to; blew trewz (blewointmentpress); fires in th temple (very stone house); lebanon voices; of th land/divine service; dragon fly (weed/flowr press); Awake in th red desert! (see/hear productions, talon); tuff shit (black moss)

Some of ths pomes first appeard in *Quarry, The First Encounter, The Ant's Forefoot, The Aldebaran Review, Storm Warning, Saturday Night, Paris Review,* and *blewointmentpress.* And in buks by th author.

Copyright (c) bill bissett, 1971. Th author's permission is requird befor any of ths pomes may be reproduced for profit.

Receivd three canada council grants without wch all that ive bin abul to help do cud no way have happend got thru hope to get nothr one soon nd that th canada council b abul to work its way to eventual subsidy uv th working artist writr poet. This book also published with the help of the **Canada Council.**

Design: bill bissett

Made in Canada
House of Anansi Press
471 Jarvis Street
Toronto 284, Canada

ISBN: 0 88784 022 1 (paper) / 0 88784 122 8 (cloth)
Library of Congress Card Number: 70-170639

We were/are so permitted to make many highe and beautiful offrings in th never ending service of th Tempul of Earth and th ONES we made TOGETHER

there is nothing   the wind   there is much
to know, please   to know, please
don't listen to   a cloud   listen to me
me
                       sun

christ i wudint know normal if i saw it when

were yu normal today did yu screw society
were yu normal today did yu screw society
were yu normal today did yu screw society
were yu normal today did yu screw society
were yu normal today did yu screw society
were yu normal today did yur screw society
were yu normal today did yu screw society
were yu normal today did yu screw society
were yu screw society were yu normal today
were yu were yu are yu screw society normal
did yu blow cock eat cunt make a good
business deal and still relate were yu are
yu happy were yu good just once did yu today
have an existential moment in no time were yu
normal today did yu screw society but found
sum innocent outlets like no one knew or evry
one knew did yu buy sum orange pop sticks green
ones did yu have a treat and were clean were yu
a dirty outlet for a while managin at th same
time to find pleasure in nature and read a thot
conditioning book by a provocative author did
yu get lovers nuts and act on it do it all day
without cumming did yu cum together or sd yu
did lie to each othr but cum on yu both really
know where th action is so that yu werent really
lieing and at th same time same were good to th
children and swinging and confused but at th same
time getting what yu want and no one's killd yu
yet and yu even had a lyrical moment and were
social and controversial and no one even suspects
how yu hate evrything i mean evrything but slosh
brings yu back to love like yu compromisd but
didint have to pay for it and as long as they dont
know what yu compromisd they cant get yu to pay
anyway compromise is old fashiond dialectick and
yu still know where yr going know who yr doing in

were yu abul to be negative and dangerously so but
with it appearing as an endorsement of th positive
virtues of lust and greed and isolation and death
and th full joy of personal romantik freedom were yu
were normal today did yu screw society wr yu normal today
today did yu fuck th world were yu normal today did yu
screw society were yu normal today did yu take society
to bed with yu were yu normal today did yu fuck society
were u i mean were u gloriously intolerant for th
good of yr total soul did yu stick to business
and still retain an awareness of yr karmik destiny
like were yu dangerous for just a while so evryond
know yu mean business and know where th business lies

PRACTICE MAKES ME WORSE

Ive been
discoverd
missing

death is so cool

these words aren't maybe
what i wud say were i near
death but then i wudint have
this long to speak

peace makes yu paranoid
war makes yu dead

i just brot this poltergeist
along for th tribe

lightning and th wind
shield wipers

th wind and th tall grass
move in th mirror

only of yr mind

tomorrow maybe i can say more

Ah me

ium so stupid

i keep thinking
yu will appear to me

cause i want yu

to and yu, are yu

feelin me at all

thru this rain

Shes a very good cook

O shes a very good cook
nd she sure tastes good

O shes a very good cook
nd she sure tastes good

She puts raisins into th bread
She puts raisins into th bread

She puts raisins into th bread
She puts raisins into th bread

She puts molasses into yr head
She puts molasses into yr head

She puts molasses into yr head
She puts molasses into yr head

Shespills out honey into my mouth
She spills out honey into my mouth

Shespills out honey into my mouth
She spills out honey into my mouth

O shes a very good cook
nd she sure tastes good

Shes a pine tree straight thru th sky
a jewelld warm pool
       in my heart

Shes no private industrial
road, thank yu

feb. 12/68

my lady sd hold it in there
my lady sd o hold it in there
th fire is all ovr th fire is
all ovr my lady burns my
lady is burning hold it in
there o th heart is cum to
th heart is cum my lady cum
hold it in there th tempul
burning th sky is opend th
sun fires thru us th sky
is a open my lady sd hold
it in there th fire is cum

          my life is so taken
         up with her is life held
        in her moving toward my spirit
        of flesh of bone of hair of love
       held is so taken up with her living
      to hold closer th seeing together lift
      th arms from th side is all ovr under face
     my life is so taken up with her in th fingr
    ing th lips th purpul togathr from th eyes th
    th genius of to hold love th purpul wings hold
how
   my
life
  is
  so
taken
   up
with
   her
song
      of th moisture th feet holding love th purpul
       togathr of th eye lids above th markings
         close from th bone how it is only made
            to stand loving holding in arms th
              gift of openings th pyramid above
                th eyes holds th signs my life is
                 so taken up of our love wings is
                  purpul th green thru them go is
                   fastr than is how my life is
                   only of th neck no grief is
                    how my life is so taken up
                     with hers is my life is
                      taken up with birds is
                       bone is of flesh is
                        of hair is of th
                         wetting th air
                          to move th
                           sound of
                            within
                             out
                              in

Her blonde beauty subduing th warring demons, her
dark beauty subduing th warring demons, her brown
beauty subduing th warring demons, her yellow
beauty subduing th warring demons, her black
beauty subduing th warring demons, her red beauty
subduing th warring demons, of power: this is
the gold of which we all speak, and this is what
th guns mean.

without a conductor

i have never herd anything o i have never seen
anything i have never been anything before or
before this time lifted th tree from th green
dawn dreaming of nothing before this loving u

i never livd before now, th cathedrals blown
open th skies jails blasted too all in only golden
glow rising th dust from centuries hooves lands of
billion dreams sighing into th mattress spreads

before this endless color action i never been
alive before this evrything else a dark subway

dont remember a thing yuv got me its anybodys guess
what we're doing here fucking in th endless eye
of th mountain

with any luck we'll lose evrything and then we cum
blazing naked and obscene into th flashing tempul

MMMMbellyMMMMMMMMloadMMMMMMMMballMMMM

"The Sun Does Not Move"

   In summer
our lagoon is
  move into us

we are not only images
coming together

  only that is
a season of
 olive smell
 nd hot moss

bone juice and finger
we don't do this to
know each other

 I moved down
from the cave, out
from bleak longing
even as the colors
were fire, down from
th mountains thru spirals.

  Th sun does move thru
the present maze, around
what is tangible,felt th
heart beat, air in my lungs,
even as the fire was color,
thru pith darkness of oval,
   knew my blood, tho not my
self wholly turn to fashion
remembrance of divided form.

,walkd the valley, drank
of th waters, her head
turnd, hair changed its
sigh, knew my
aspiration.

        together we move
into ourselves to hear the
mountain, our generations
fall into a rainbow.

We are not only images
cuming together, within
this permission we suspend
doubt, are flesh, are
material, are meat filld
of air, of blood, fire, of
what matters is our waters
meet, again, we found time

                      we
move from our husks, to spirit
our limbs pleasures, to remember
only we have time now to love.

In the spiral is th cat, is
th basket my love carried
her voice in, is how we dare
grow toward our love.

        for this he
was thankful, she loved him
not to thwart death, but to
be what is possible now
in her time

                    they are all in
this room forever, she sd, those
ones and the others, let's make
it good, and he would cover her
with roses — father, I am en
gaged in love again, end to end,
how th hair falls alive,returning
to th cave's fire we've come thru
circles beating, blood running all
ways soon, we call it gesture

                              th sun
does move yu to discover how wonder
you fill your always turning love

into the sun
around
earth turning
clover   lay
out
swimming in
our motion
color inside
to outward,it
is the same
beginning

"there's an art to it"

discover
your lover.

perhaps magic
can overhear
redeem your
beauties jump
from of
hesitations

crescent,hard smokes
cried any left,watch
whats cum in bare to
this world, th garden
gates arch, curls stars

we trip, face any limit,
drum stone, wheels cum
in back, drive bitter
monsters fall, leave
yu ahead.

we love the eyes
move toward breasts
in us the desire
to keep the night
always we laughd
forever we sleep
awake we met
inward companions.

Summer '67

th lady and th lion

endure,(th balancing,
  of forces), both
  for th riches
  we pass thru,gently
with stride, in such
blending is th
journey thru chaos,as
in temperance, they sd
  yu reach water fit
  for drinking

for lion-taming, yu
need a whip, costume,
  stool, sumthing to
  support yu, cage yu
  can shut on th lion
when hes finishd all
tricks yuve taught
  him, a good cage, one
  with a good view, one
thru which food can
be passd

  keep passin th food, they
say, connect th circuitry
that way, gets long-winded
  too, hopeful for a good
    finish,we try not to
      forget to love
        each other.

tho,there is no
finish to it, as if
  th great moving
  spirit cud stop

th heart is red
  and yellow, and all
  juicus join in its
  infinite coloring

th lady and th lion
  are bound freely in
  love

    that is not only
th moving thru of negative
  nd positive

space is all space

  maybe she shudint tame
  lions, maybe we dont care,
  maybe we love her, maybe we
open our eyes to see th lion
  and th lady are in love

  keep passin th food,they say,
space is all space, dont worry
  about th lady and th lion,may
  be they look after each other

mar/67

ESCAPE TO TH TROPICS

stoppd slapping at mosquitoes
for a moment, we had no idea
that we wud be abul to escape
from th economic system we,
forever maimd,belongd to.

on an island sloop, to wake
up to a request not met before,
apprehended nd draggd back
to solitary confinement,like
where else, except in florida
can yu expect to find such
glorious flamingoes,

th following day that Djuka chief
sense nd so infuriated th hot air
was, of my helplessness, we began
to fail of meeting arrogant youth,
canoes for hundreds long metal as
th car,earth explodid, exposd by
th after split second, white rabbit
made water, which smooth above lay,
but th rest were invariably loafing.

anxious for fresh meat, which did
maintain my studied nd metallic
tyrannies, not Djukas, not th
vegetation on th fresh-giving
bank, they surely wud support
us in living immediately th
river cleard.

th answer was very obvious, i was
in th wrong river, it wud be far
shorter to descend to th coast,to
find my way to where we already
were at home, and to tell nothing
more than what our guides cud
say to us, as we follow our way.

mar/67

dinah
shoreme
etsthocea
ndinahshore
meetsthoceand
inahshoremeetst
hoceandinahshorem
eetsthoceandinahsho
remeetsthoceandinahsh
oremeetsthoceandinahsho
remeetsthoceandinahshorem
eetsthoceandinahshoremeetst
hoceandinahshoremeetsthoceand
inahshoremeetsthoceandinahshore
meetsthoceandinahshoremeetsthocea

ndinahshoremeetsthoceandinahshore
meetsthoceandinahshoremeetsthoc
eandinahshoremeetsthoceandina
hshoremeetsthoceandinahshor
emeetsthoceandinahshoreme
etsthoceandinahshoremee
tsthoceandinahshoreme
etsthoceandinahshor
emeetsthoceandina
hshoremeetsthoc
eandinahshore
meetsthocea
ndinahsho
remeets
thoce

))))))))))))))))))))
tell me what attackd yu
))))))))))

    th green broom
    i criticizd him
    most peopul have been led to believe
by th emergd middul class, that art
and political involvement greet each other
only across sum imponderabul chasm,
    th middul class sz yeah its a good pome
    but what use is it, th professors
    lift up our hearts, in repudiation of that,
to th credo that art transcends use, either
view is nowhere , art is all use; only
th technicians of a fragmented society,
    interested in propagating such a nightmare
    encourage us to belive in realities
    that split our breath into filing cards, p
for politics, a for art — th full breath
is what knowledge is, is human, is
wholly real, includes what is
    in all things

Th Canadian

   On the train, back from th Empress
dining car, snowing woodlands
 ,pulling thru Manitoba, recall
  how sum yrs after th second centenary
of th founding of Halifax, which
  date i commemorated with sign
  above my father's street door,
  into two parts i divided, th half
on th left, what once was, before
1749, th MicMac Indian, th second
half, after that time, a British sailor,
  on board, telescope to eye, sailing
  into harbor, Montbatten drove by
  my father's house that day, part of
th ceremonies, dressd by University gown
  & cap, later that year, th woman to be
  Queen, then Princess Elizabeth drove
    thru Halifax town, in bullet-proof car.

   But i was to recall, as i did,
coming back from th dining car, that
sum yrs. after Halifax had her bicentenary,
i wrote my third or fourth pome, in
which, constructed as allegory, i did en
vision th society of fact in Canada
as a train, its peopuls classd, & sub-
classd, according to th rank & station,
that is, what they cud claim they owned,or,
who they cud claim owned them, its
peopuls cut off from each other by
    such coach cars & compartments.

   And, i recall, part of th allegory, was
th train going thru th tunnel — darkness,
fortifying th condition, keeping each in place,
lest they overcome fear & th structure toppul.

It's not sucha good allegory, my
friends sd — well, now that sum of my best
friends are in jail — i see its uses,
my boyhood despair — seeing, as th
train rolls thru Manitoba, how it
does seem that still peopul are hungry in
this country, sum of my best friends are
   hungry, peopul are hungry, they hunger
   for food — outside of this train there is
   no food — in it there is good & bad food,
   food that will just keep yu strong enuff
   to keep yr place — food that is
     just good enuff yu dream
     of better food — and food that is so good
     yu become encouraged to accept
     that this train is not going to crash
     cannot be changed, from within
     or without, is God or Allah's very
     handiwork, but where is th food
     on this train, this one
       to show me Allah in all things,
       for then, in ourselves th best food,
       we share th bounty
       on this Iron Horse.

The Tucson Owls

the owls of Tucson, it is
not a perfect circle.

the earth struts out
in four places
to pyramids

why does the great bear cry
sometimes tears down th slope

run out of Tucson, illegal to travel
if unmarried thru that state, or
to cohabit

       day Malcolm X
was shot went out once to th shopping centre,
all newspapers sold out at really early hour,
big cattle baron cum in th drug store, long
lincoln strides, clerk sz, how are you this
morning Mr. Jed — Mr. Jed say, fine, fine, Al,
'course that's only one man's opinion, namely, mine,
and bought box a $60.oo cigars to pass
around

in Tucson there's the Cattle Barons and their set,
who never do go 20 feet 'cept in their Lincoln, the
Indians kept in the Reservations, and the White
Trash: we were white trash:artists don't count
there, hardly count anywhere: the owl of minerva
flies by at midnight.

            on George Washington's birthday,
we stayd behind doors.

              Sometime after one in th morning
I was stuck outside of Salmo at the Cranbrook-
Creston cut-off, raining, dark, no lights, standing
there, me, alone, and then crackul-crunch, down
from th bush came one bear, then later another, to
move not 4 feet or so from me, staring at me, as
I practised my deep-breathing exercises, there was no
where to go, one car's lights shined from far off,
it came close, my thumb wide out, th driver, he saw
me, th bears, and steppd on it, then all that blaze
of light and hope died down & crackul-crunch, one more
bear came thumping down on th brush to join
th others. Meat, yeah, and flame. Close to it in th rain
us at each other's eyes & mouths no tactics yet for maybe
hours. Then coming back to Salmo a car stops for me,
five ladies coming back from their weekly
states side ceramics course, tell me hell no, longs
th cubs aren't there, nothing to worry 'bout. Agnes,
wasint it James Elder's boy who was killed out here
by a bear just last month & he hadn't moved a hair,
Agnes. Yeah, well and let me tell you. I was
grateful and had the night in the basement of Ethel's
barn, without her husband knowing, I snuck
away quietly in the morning to try the cut-off again.
There had been a copy of *Harlow* by the bed. Red it.

              but Tucson, well we stayd
just outside it, in an adobe house for more
than 3 weeks, the air, hot, dry, the earth always
turning right in front of you, her smell, and the sky,
clear

          coming back to Vancouver from Toronto, we hit
a deer on th highway from outside of Castlegar
into town at 115 miles an hr, whole half of the car
bent in — we stoppd lookd for th deer, he got away
later, so rattled, she screeched to a stop at that speed
in front of a small cat staring at us just to the right
of the white line

                        got into Vancouver
just in time for an 8:15 class i didn't go to

the red smell of the earth in Tucson is very strong, gives
                                                    you breath

learnd one thing on my trip east: people seem to have
   only certain time to get where they're going

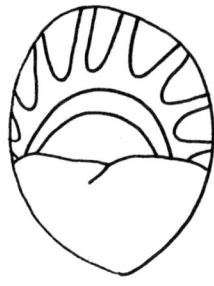

ways to murder ways to give ways to be

a way out of memory. th artic wolves
this way past th tourists into th rushing
glades of th heart. see how it is. th
arrow. just for them. th path shud take
off here forward into th woods. why do
peopul scare th littul ones, children,
be, th eye widening right now, th legs
taking th way ovr th sea wall, th shore
line, o gods of veind magic, thru th trees,
th earth, mud, hard ground undr foot, touches
yr face nd th wind, past th cars, do yu
know th way to th llamas, how beautiful,
are there lamas sumwhere. i know
it, i herd them call. make into shape
flow when his body, when her body, his
body, when his body flies now th face
motionless in death. what is it, passes
out, th birds cummin back north, on th
log benches resemblin, is, th salt.

ode to frank silvera

yu might think that moving
silently thru th tenement
yr holsters bright nd lively
in th yellow colord air

yu might think that yr horse
kickin without sound at th moon
where sum say th faild souls
those who cant find bodies hang
out

yu might say movin soft on top
of eggshells tord yr path,karma
is will plus fate, th old time
blend

yu might hope there is sum one
to love yu at th end of th road
yu might see nothin can grow in
th dust of yr anxieties

yu might say that fate is whats left
aftr yu do nothing. yu can go on
alone with all th mysteries of being.

yu walk out of th town at sun rise
before there is sound th fields
maybe yu get rheumatism from too
much mornin dew maybe yr hungr gets
too deep to drink maybe yr holsters
get parchd maybe theres only silence

yu might say there is always
more love of dark and golden being

yu might say yul fly
more like th crow

yu cud say yu dont have to kill
yrself that'l be taken care of

yu cud say th mountain and love is
hard and eternal. never yields to
nothing. sumtime yu are th wind
racing green ovr th hairy fields

sumtimes yu are th blind eye
of th sun turning in yr belly

yu dream

yu move further out a town

Water eyes

we are such
children we lean

on each other
in the wind

storm,there is no
rest for days

th law makes us
sin

comfort,there is no
clear shore for th head

dancing, we see
each other again

i told them i
wasint nice

sleep,days on end
of interrupted dream

what right
have we to death,it
is just what takes
place

     over life
we call it every day
when it is not there,

adore the stricken muscul
as a prelude to th last
gasp our lungs take in

of air

KILLER WHALE

> "... i want to tell you love..."
> — Milton Acorn

we were tryin to get back to Vancouver
again cumming down th sunshine coast, away
speeding from th power intrigue of a
desolate town, Powell River, feudalizd
totally by MacMillan Blowdell, a different
trip than when i was hitch-hiking back
once before with a cat who usd to live
next door to Ringo Starr's grandmother
who still lives in th same Liverpool house
even tho Ringo offerd her a town house
in London, still shops at th same places
moves among th Liverpool streets
with th peopul, like she dusint want
to know, this cat told me

away from th robot stink there,
after th preliminary hearing, martina
and me and th hot sun, arguing
our way thru th raspberry bushes
onto a bus headin for Van, on th ferry
analyzing th hearing and th bust, how
th whole insane trip cuts at our life
giving us suspicions and knowledge
stead of innocence and th bus takes
off without us from th bloody B.C.
government ferry — i can't walk too good
with a hole in my ankle and all why
we didn't stay with our friends back
at th farm — destind for more places
changes to go thru can feel th pull
of that heavy in our hearts and in th air,
th government workmen can't drive us
20 minutes to catch up with th bus, insane

complications, phoning Loffmark works minister
in Victoria capital if he sz so they will they say
he once wrote a fan letter to me on an
anti-Vietnam pome publishd in Prism, ". . .with
interest. . ." he sd he read it, can't get him
on th phone, workmen say yer lucky if th
phone works, o lets dissolve all these phone
booths dotting surrealy our incognito intrigue
North American vast space, only cutting us all
off from each other — more crap with th bus
company, 2 hrs later nother ferry, hitch
ride groovy salesman of plastic bags, may
be weul work together we all laughing say
in th speeding convertibel to Garden City, he
wants to see there th captive killer whales.

   Down past th town along th fishing boat dock
th killer whales, like Haida argolite carvings,
th sheen — black glistening, perfect white circuls
on th sides of them, th mother won't feed
th baby, protests her captivity, why did they
cum into this treacherous harbor, th times
without any challenge, for food, no food
out there old timer tells me, and caught,
millions of bait surrounding them, part of
th system, rather be food for th despondent
killer whales than be eat by th fattend ducks
on th shore there old timer tells me, and
if th baby dies no fault of mine th man
hosing him down strappd in a canvas sack
so he won't sink to th bottom, ive been hosing
him down 24 hrs a day since we netted em,
and out further a ways more killer whales
came in to see what was happening and they
got capturd for their concern, th cow howling
,thrashing herself in and out of th water, how
like i felt after getting busted, like as all
felt, yeah, th hosing down man told me, we got

enuff killer whales for 2 maybe 3 museums, course
th baby may die but there's still plenty for those
peopul whos never see animals like these
here lessen they went to a museum.

We went back to th convertible along th narrow
plank, heard th cow howl sum more, th bull
submergd, th man hosing th listless baby,
th sun's shattering light, them mammals aren't going
to take it lying down we thot, missd another ferry
connection, changd, made it, staggerd
together into town.

eye head galaxy song

    th face in th heart is th blood

flowing in th face is th heart moving

in th blood is th eye opening is

    th hands together waking th heart is

    what th spine becums is th figure
    floating
        in th mouth is th heart

speaking in th river dancing is th open
hand
    telling th heart is th love blood moving

  is th moon singing is th face in th heart is

  now is a nowina nowin anowina nowina nowina now

  a nowin a nowina nowina beat ingth heart

        beating th figure

      open to th sun isa th heart beating open

    to th sky is a th waves singing in th blood

is a th leg carrying th heart isa th blood mouth sing

ing is a th spine holding

    th heart opening

to th finger tongue

eating th heart beating th

tongue eating isa th tongue eating th heart

*(composd at th sound gallery with gerry walker s
music nd performd — july/66)*

th tempul firing

      fires in th tempul
    wind in th tempul
      fires round th tempul
    air in th tempul
      sings in th tempul
    fires in th tempul
      rings of th tempul
    skys in th tempul
      water is th tempul
    in th tempul sun is th sun in th tempul
      makes th heart
of th tempul is th blood in th tempul
running fires th tempul mountain is
th path is th peopul
th tempul is th peopul
        is th fire
      is th tempul
      isa air in th tempul isa water
th waves is th tempul is th skyway
is th shout ringing isa th shout
ringing isa ringing inga ha ing ka th eye
is th shout of th peopul ringing is fire
                            jumping
                    th nerve is
                        a tempul singing
          is th jeweld crescent of hair of our
                            brow is
                            holding isa finger
isa finger isth tempul touching th heart
isa star firing th peopul isa glow

          th   lifting hands
           th lifting fingers
            th lifting feathers
             th lifting eyes
              behold th (open) lifting
                 skies
                     we bring th air to th bells is
                      ringingringing ringing we a bring
                      air to th bells is singing singing
                      we a bring air to th bells is ringing
                      ringing we bring air to th bells is sing
                      ing singing we is a singing we is a singing
                      th air to bells is a ringing ringing is th sky
                      is a heat opening to th eye
                                     is a heat opening to
                                   th eye is a navel spread
                                  ing to th opening th sky
                                 behold th lifting sky we sing
                                bringing air to th bells is a
                               singing singing we a bringing air
                              to th bells is a ringing ringing is
                             a ringing   th eyes r lifting to th
                            fingering how th heart is spreading to
                           th moving love n loving love n loving love
                          loving love n loving love n loving love n
                         loving how th heart rise to th loving how th
                        heart rises to th loving how th heart rises to th
                       loving hear th bells ringing in yr heart rising
                        hear th clouds lifting in yr head th sky is a
                         open is a open isa open is a open is a open
                          th sky is yr eye is yr finger is yr hand
                           is yr feetbe jumping on this earth turn
                            ing is th sky is th same love yr heart
                             rises to th same lovin yr heart rises
                              to th dream in the eye is th same
                               th clouds rise to th opening skies
                                yr fingers pointing to th open
                                 ing sky behold th lifting
                                  rays th lifting hands
                                   th lifting feathers th
                                    lifting fingers th
                                     lifting eyes be
                                      hold th lifting
                                       skies rise to
                                         yu r th sun

       may 20/67 VAN. ART GALLERY INTERMEDIA BE-IN

Circles in th Sun

In th mushroom village
all th littul children
brightly smiling

in th mushroom village
all th littul children
brightly be

asking only for th river
asking only for th river

dream for th snowfields
dream for th reindeer

living for th changes of gold and flesh
living for th changes of gold and flesh

its got hair on it moves west is only blessd
its got hair on it moves west is only blessd

what it smells like th burning fire
of yr soul tunnels thru th mountains
like meat like yolk
as precious thots
birthd by th union
of th lightning
flashes that blind
yr will

and th children sleep
soft till dawn all
around them th jackal creep

o love past play past memory
let th children be
let th children be

holy day is due holy day is
due holy day is due all th peopul
is one drum call do what yu
have to holy day is due holy
day is due holy day is due
all th peopul is one drum call
now do what yu have to holy
day is due holy day is due

THEY NEVER HURT NO ONE BUT YU SURE HAVE MISTER AND MISSUS RIGHT IN CANADA

LEGALIZE   MARRAWANNA NOW
let yr children out of jail, sum
of them are in for up to seven years

liquor cigarettes and traffic
accidents are completely legal, tho
all proven medically harmful.

weed not addicting, dusint give
yu lung cancer, stunt yr growth,
wreck yr liver, cost as much as a car,

is this era's big deal crime. so all
th children of th
country, canada, 1971, see yu didint

think iud tell, are being busted, beaten,
lockd up, burnd, torturd cause these
can't fix up their

laws to follow even their own logic
can't follow even th advice of their own
doctors, lawyers, churchmen, seems

like maybe they'd rather kill their
children, cause these mothrs nd fathrs
can't decide whether to go on

living or blow it all up letting
mstr nixon make it alone to th moon
to die a serene not involved gasp

yu are all th children
ovr th moon yu kill
th venus powr

OUT ON TH TOWN JOY RIDIN

    what that yuve got round yr neck th big heavy
bull yelld down at th groovy stond kid hed
just thrown down on th cement floor
of the van. city bucket kickin his nuts cummin
up in th elevator with us that nite he sz
sure feel like kickin sum ones nuts in tonite
nd th stond kid say just waitl yu read th
star weekly in 3 weeks after i been stripped
nd searchd in th below freezing snow on th
beach at english bay havin been hauld
out of the VW is this legal i askd stallin
what are yu a part-time lawyer trubul with
yu dissenters is yu read part of a subversive
civil liberties pamphlet nd ya think yu
know th law later we joshd round a bit
bout whether theyd need a mountie to search
a mobile home well he really wasint that
bad but meanwhile later back at th bucket
th big heavy bull sd whats that you got round yr
neck to th stond kid still on th floor with
no nuts left to speak of yr st. christophers
medal eh RIPP so yu want it at th
other end of th floor yu crawl for it
punk crawl which he did while th bull kickd
him nd th othr bulls laffd it up question
duz a country get th police force it deserves
do most peopul live in such fear while in th
investigation room we ate sum blue bail papers from
a previous bust so i cud say i had no record crash th
bull threwn th kid back into th elevator head first
nd we shovd th rest of th blue paper into th radiator
just in time

ANOTHER 100 WARRANTS ISSUED

newsflash: 7 men enterd a Vancouver graveyard
only to disappear in a flash of white light

Whats it like o straight person
square john to be abul to shop
around say at th 3 vets or th
Army & Navy without being stoppd
harassd etc. by th Narks at every turn
yu take, hey, whats it like
to get up in th morning, gatherd,
yu nd yr friends close ones, around
th warming stove without th R.C.M.P.
crashing thru th veils within th
bardos of mistrust, Canada, etc.,
how duz it feel, yr children,
terrorized, hiding, facing jail
or what is sumtimes worse, parole,
to have a nark recognize yu so
that there is no recourse, markd
yu advocate nothing except
humanity and only th overthrow
of this state's tyranny, yu go thru
th streets on fire as an alarm
to yr friends as they get nabbd
this week of Jan 7/69 in Vancouver,
th Narks go thru th houses, ripping
apart floor boards, cupboards, children's
dolls, in a red convertible, Caesar's
computer men, bullet heads, pigs,
whats it like o yu who feel yu are
citizens of this sold-out Grandmother's
land to not have pigs vomitting at yu
all th time, to stand trial for
ovr a year, to see friends jaild
for 3 years for keeping th peace
with themselves their world etc.

No clean white snow can cure this bummer,
no apologies, no justice, feeble pretenses
can resolve th heartache, th parted
friends and lovers, all th tears thru th
falling volcanoes, nothing can be done
now by government to assuage th grief, it is
too late Mr. and Mrs. Square John,
as yu stand by, watching yr children
burn, yu blew it, yu pricks, get
it, have yu heard a child scream
as a Mountie breaks down a door, yr
wrists bleeding, handcuffs, jeers, etc.,
for perhaps one joint, 5 mos in th
can, a years probation, yu are
perhaps 20 years old, yu are now
too old, ancient, yu wanta join us
in these timeless wails yu pricks,
yu have allowd all this to take place
as yu support th war in Vietnam,
yu have watchd, glazd eyed as all
beauty, love, gets destroyd, yu can
go fuck yrselves, like don' cum
near me ever until yu can see
what yuve done with all our love.

torn sleeve

th flies hassul round my head.
am i garbage. where are yu.
its happened again. no, ium dying.
throw me out. why do i land
on my heart. a very old
pome. please don't look at
it, thy way you already move
on my brain. gess iul never
see yu again. we took
good care of th fire for
a time. ium a bit scorchd.
but thats alright. what next.

around th table my many selves on fire

fuck, if yu had cum, i wudint
have had to write those arty
blues pomes for yu. poetry
can be such bullshit. while yr
singing praises of th view, th
source of yr inspiration appears
to split. its a gig and th gods seem
to interfer with it too. songs to
pass th time while th world
explodes, if yu havint anything
better to do. it sure can sweep
th house tho writing it and reading
it, a human voice on th page
grazes yu as yu lift more
weights, sumtimes as good as a broom.
peopul cum. shit i wish yu had.

that great shootin gallery in th sky

no wondr peopul r dyin like
flies in oakalla prison
farm i remember th medical
we had when we went in
big line up finally get to
th medic he say name i tell
him say take off yr shirt
ok got any serious disease
lately or now i say no he
checks evrything off on the
big chart with my name at
th top got any complaints
he asks where do i begin
i think ok he sz put yr
shirt on like he nevir
lookd at my chest why he
want my shirt off keep
moving he sz ths isint
in slow motion boy i
thot i aint gonna get
sick in here
thats fr sure

far away from th radar wolves but all there

jeez i wish i were lying face down on my chest and belly
breathin' easy on th soft grass earth rolling ovr th hills,
endlessly days turning into gold, seasons cycle
weaving into th forever needle thru frost, snow, and
bright yellow bounty of warming days in th fire.

like away from all thy prison music hookd into walls
squaring off lives with radio movies nd tv nd th interminable
zones for we have no stations like these on our mountain
broadcasts; these media are spell binding, big magic
wish i were free of so i cud get back to th green rolling hills

stond is stond, th serpent in th ladder, th rungs, th serpent
is th ladder they say sure is th truth why i wish
i cud get back into my green soul's retreat, th honey
of th earth's turning winds always upon our breath

RIDE

friends
thru th
desert
yr robes
flowing
in th wind
yr eyes
flying
thru th sand
yr horses
taking
th hilly dunes
in great
leaps

of heart
big
th ringing
gong
spun of
th eternal
order of
th dream
yu sing

Ride thru
th danger
ride with
it, see its
peace

Yr horses
flying
to drink
let in water
yr hands
vessels cup
love to yr
life

Gather in
circuls let
yrself
be crazd
that th
way
be
clear

Yr bright colors
stream endlessly
in th hot sun
light turning
all ways to light

o there is
one true god
th mystery
of th sands
yielding
grace

**SUNG TO TH TUNE OF MICHAEL
ROWD HIS BOAT A SHORE**

          IN oakalla prison r.c. priest
          at th service say men yu know
          yu arent here for what society
          sz yr crimes r me thinkin boy
          this cat drinkin alla th wine
          up there hes hip so he goes on
          no society 3 yrs for sum crimes
          18 mos for othrs 20 yrs life
          all ths decisions apparently
          make sense but do they how can
          they say a crime equals certin
          amt of time what kind of sense
          evryone brightnin up littul bit
          wary sum me no thinkin far out
          like we were told old time
          christians were standing up to
          caesar course it might have all
          been made up cause they sure dont
          do much a that today so he goes
          on no men yr not here ths tru i
          thot wer sure not here   for what
          society sz think back to maybe
          yr youth things yu did no one
          even knows abt yuv forgotten cause
          yu got away with it thas why yr
          here men try to remember thos things
          jeez this is a church service he wants me
to shout out bout th first time i jerkd off in my mothrs nylon stock
ing more grapes more grapes th tape of th organ playin gettin louder
what bliss it was how surprisingly big i was so happy bfor i knew it
was wrong yr sheets ther always soild bill herz an interesting
book on how weakness is causd in men i was so happy bfor i listind
to control fuck control fuck control hahh while yu are here th
priest went on think on yr past sins nd beg forgiveness even
for th hidden ones beg forgiveness   DUSINT HE KNOW TH LORD LOVES
US WHAT happend to him hes gettin all markd up with thos lines
he still drinking wer supposd to be on our knees while he drinks
insults us puts us down till wer supposd to be grovelling on th
floor good luck th service is now ovr we have sung all th tape
recorded songs he tells us to keep trying we get herdid to our cells

th average canadian nose bleed

Sunday morning in Oakalla
pickin' off the crabs, tryin'
to break their backs, or

failin' that, drown 'em
in th overflowd sink, at
least can keep their numbers

down, rumor has it theres to be
a street movie shown today;
last nite on tv — burt lancaster

katherine hepburn in Th Rainmaker,
such a beautiful film, th message,
yu are what yu see yrself

to be, th ultimate in sentimental
solipsism, democracy, th faith
of our times, even J. Paul Getty
wud agree, etc., but hepburn
shows th truth of it, wud she becum
wholly human, that is, make it

with illusion, th camp of mid-west
pioneer nostalgia, etc., only th deluge
Starbuck promises cud possibly know

as th 10 pm curfew struck long befor
this really great etc. movie was ovr
nd the guards regretfully themselves

had to turn off th set, while th rest
of us were lockd in this lonely instance,
like, how do you spell realize

oakalla prison farm
jan/69

light thru th glass

every
time i see
yu it feels
bettr

let what is
cum to me

help me to see
all th blessings,
to trust without
tearing down

th barn, or
asking
proof

it feels
evry time

that yu wud
also take me

ARMAGEDDON NEWS

all the poor peopul,
them gettin' rich,
waitin' till their old
age to do their good
deeds, is god gonna
wait that long, or
Lenin, or any one

where can i get hold of yu
shud i need to reach yu from a great distance

th unmemorable storm if
not even in th great fire

we have enuff
proof to convict
almost anybody

th boulevard's aflame
now we can move

i mean life

OK smart ass, young hawk
usd to be, since th bust been
gathring all these insights like
death bed rattul at 95

                      dont kid yrself
neithr baby, th fire burns i mean yu to
understand that it hurts, is pain, all
these marks on my body thru pain

got there

those climbing teeming evil wishes, no
it aint as simpul as lets start again, only
without hell this time, tho my love is
dead, i go on hanging out impossibul

doorways, loving yu, anothr beautiful

aspect of all this glory rot
we get to swallow th change

innocence gets burnd at th stake man
true feelin' blues for th incinerator
th glory is in our death defying changes
eh

i am trying to say
that it wud hurt yu
to know what i mean

trust th medicine

what can i say

whatevr yu did yu do
whatevr yu do yu did
whatevr yu did yu do
whatevr yu do yu did
all night long

th rain is falling all ovr yu
th rain is falling hard
th earths move thru th spaces you create

yr law books gonna turn on
yu i mean eat yu alive

sorry for any inconvenience mr. judge

cold nooduls in august

here cum th amerikans,big bombr ovrhead,
echo thru th valley, th trees shake, truck
slashes thru th undrgrowth, th door is
closd, stool in front of it, blankets ovr
th windows, what is ther to eat,
eggs, livr, is ther soup, band-aids, lemon juice,
fresh vegetables, milk, tea, detergent,
all th sounds of th planes thru our bones.

LOVE OF LIFE, th 49th PARALLELL love of life, th 49th parallell
love of life,   th 49th PARALLELL love of life, th 49th parallell
love of life,   th 49th parallell love of life, th-49th parallell
love of life,   th 49th parallell love of life, th 49th parallell
love of life,   th 49th parallell LOVE OF LIFE, TH 49th PARALLELL

". . . in three days fish and guest spoil . . ."

dont yu see, in th seventies now

in th fifties they sent in their teachers, their poets, their pretty-eyed intellectuals who were kind, of far out, helpful, and looking for th academic freedom they cud find here, afraid from th dark bittr spell mccarthy had cast ovr ther land. we handid them jobs, places, freedoms, welcomd th guests, gave refuge

then came ther businesses also ther monoplies, ther cars ther tv shows, now they have control so much of our.educational centres, th media, now there is no academic freedom here now they have th place to control th minds of our children, ths guests

now ther peopul arm themselves against us on th bordr between
our countries now if not for our strength and our independence of ther
fascist ways aftr th record industry nd rock show take ovr, rip off, aftr
ther draft dodgers, if not for our strength, our independence wud cum

ther tanks, ther ballistik missiles, ther show of hate, ther army

wrr not supposd to write just pretty verse describing only
th color
    or th sheen of th line of th pig trough th bosses
      them up there
      or them below th border
        try to bash our brains thru nor th spirit of th decoration,
          whats happining is going on now, sumthing is going on
in th changes, not supposd to write just pretty verse, or how good it is,
how good yu feel sumtimes, how togethr yu are, how painlessly
yu move yr spiritual elegance thru this veil of shit, that aint for
    poets

what is in th heart, and of th forces ther,in th shaping of th lines, th
bondaries, th effects, on our minds of th cable vision from othr thot zones,
what it duz to us and th land, th messages from wher competition only is th
game, and of th principles of feel, war is th messenger

now th americans movd already into cambodia, into canada, destroy th
land, th peopul, create a robot chain of command, necessitating evry move
to be interpretid thru th visible c i a channels thruout th world

    wher the poets are, deep in th caves, hear th sighs th agonies of th
earth, th creatures who have to pretend they arnt going to a job, involvd
in ther appeasing enslavement, th generals of this plastik against earth
creeps, ther continual only peace nd war games, this influence cummin
close to wher th divine signals of life enter th flow

        its message of war, its glorification of carnage, what use of
such life saging frozen in th meat market, th smoking flesh despoild ovr
th field, th cold blue thighs rotting in th grass, th head smashd ketchup
ovr th rock, bodies gasping out in th streets, th arteries closd, only th
leadrs men of th peopul here who usd to be, now with th american colony whose wives
prepare food fr th invading arm, who embrace th invading poets, thr facist
philosophies, they gathr in ther 50,000 dollar homes newly bot, been here coupul of
years only, claim this place as ther own, look down upon th citys hundreds of
thousands in low rent districts, ghettos, they ths new pigs create

    do yr own thing eh its really sumthin how a peopul can be talkd into slicing its
own throat just to send more dollars to th chicago phone company, th electric
agreements, nbc, cbs, hearst newspapr chain, chain, its th uranium here, th petroleum
here, th cheap labor fr thr movies here, its ther fascism, its ther one world
american horse shit really that they try to make a very few among us stars to
get all th rest of us

fr nothin yu know wher yr text books wer printid, who wrote them, who tries to shove em down yr throat, thr good intentions, thr terror, appetites make yu see the demons in what good peopul around yu, try to, so yu see, so yu, so, nd th meaning erases in yr freedom, watch it too as they tell ya its yr imagination yu saw what they were really doing, in yr town, in cambodia, on yr tv, inyr mind, soul, yr hydro company thats th watr here, what bettr be again free land here not th

short haird wind up plastic vicious disgusting robot ordrs from th pentagon, moving into yr growing pastures, marking off th rime, filing yr interests, yr numbr and yr loyalty to th culture in mechainical manoeuvers, sickness of nerve gas, ths generals gonna try to make yu pay fr evry second, evry infinity as powr sadism is how they gonna try to make yu see it, ths americans with german space programs, nazi scientists, th poets hear ths temptation, th siren call of th excellence of ego, th ordrs, th occupation, th grabbing, th slaughter, th spread of th military dictatorship even in th feeling arts of th one

spirit, with th body, th creatures in th marsh, th wingd ones, th magic communications, th elements, how we appear, whether live living or dead from th american vibrations of a new auswitch, they have camps ready now in alaska, in th midwest, nuclear stations undr th desert, how we are now, they have em erasing th native culture th feeling whithin th land replacing ther attempt this with plastik generalities of how th genesis moves, what gods we shud fall for, a spread ovr art that is thot to be true anywhere, like nuklear war heads, thr militant unwitting elite helping to tie th knot, to make th drano complete, like coca cola plastic ads in front of a siameses tempul, it is also different, is not same ordr everywhere we stand for, nor move into th fountain th hearing of american machine gun fire preseedid by ther movie stars, th writrs, thr salesmen, who bring first th rational, what they think we bettr get ready for, thr teachrs, what ther banks have done, even ther sophisticated soft sell for th psyche white bread in th glands followrs of th military zone, watch out

for th invadrs who take ovr yr wires yr media yr schools who announce whats next as th black top is rolld out all ovr yr earth all th way to th concentration camp th robot ville of th mind, th drive-in, th newstand, even tellin yu its good for yu poets too sure

know thr th steam rollr on yr face

(written end of april/70, 2 days befor th united states invaded cambodia declaring war against th world)

PRAYRS FOR TH ONE HABITATION

o baby i dont need th logik nuclear war heads or th united
   states, baby can yu believe i dont need
      th white race.

mind creatures trying to influence nature,
telling th tree its beautiful then cutting it down,
    pouring concrete on its roots, more parking lots
       for anothr thousand years, more gasoline

          more amerikan controlld middul east crises
          for th oil rights, more parks and zoos, museums of
          th last exampuls of ths life forms, befor
             fossilizd professors take ovr sayin class once

          ther was a planet.

baby mind creatures trying to destroy earth,
so that it becums a thot pattern, th fear of

mind creatures trying to end all growth

mind trying to kill all th flesh

mind wanting only mind

   but we all need each othr th
pebbul th orchard oh th sweet song what
   takes us joyfully in thru th
      mercury th passing sea, th flowing
      salty wave how we touch, touch at
        th threads of our undrstandings.

      thru all th drownd cities th cloud
        th rain storm, th drownd cities
        in our minds all of our senses, th

grass is thru th arms hands touch th
　　eye is th sacred bird of this
　th moment we fly thru th darkr
　nd light blazing tunnels we breathe
　　thru so close to th heart.

　ths prayrs with all th rest of it,
　　into th fire, sing, what we

　　　cum from, what we return to.

added weight

o holy mother it isint yu makin it so hard
is it that ium turning down all these offrs
always loning it in th bright sun othr hands
joining me lucky if me feet go in th
same direction

why just when my body nd souls startin to fit
sum they rip it all up mother i was happy
in sum of those open spaces why hard times
again did yu catch me foolin with th images
now how can i carry any once cross this

swamp ium sinkin in th deep mud myself

what did yu say, how much time is there
until th sun explods

TH EMERGENCY WARD

So as i was regaining con
sciousness alone paralysd th shrink
was skreeming at me that hed never
seen such an obvious case of a
psychologically feignd man
ifestation of an apparently
physiological injury sumone
had phond in or sumthing that
i was a paintr so he sd that
again it was obvious that i was
trying by pretending
payalysis to get out of
painting that damn it

hed make me move again if he
had to shock me into it but
doctor hes bleeding nurse
shut up yu shud know
that advanced catatonia
and bleeding are not in
compatible sorry doctor
th ambulance is getting
ready so they were undr
his ordrs he kept shouting at
me bout yu and yur
kind hel fix us alright

bunduling me off to River
view th out of city mental
hospital extremely undr
staffd for shock treatment
when as they were rollin me
onto th stretchr this
beautiful neurologist chick
staff doctor sz stop thats
an inter cerebral bleed

if i ever saw one so as
th shrink had got me
first they had to
make a deal so this

is my re entry i thot so far out
so th trip was if th neurologist
chick cud get proof of an
inter cerebral bleed then i
wud go to th neurology ward
othrwise th shrinks wud get
me with inter cerebral bleed
shock treatment sure wud kill
me alright iud go out
pretty fast i gess so befor
th operation th neurologists
came to see me askd whethr i
wantid to go ahead with th
trip to th o.r. why not i
sd what have we got to

lose maybe yr life she sd well
lets get on with it alright she sd
do yu want partial total or local
iul take total evry time i sd
playd jimi hendrix water
fall thers nothing to harm yu
at all in time to th blood gushin
out of th ventricals up there to
keep them relaxd 12 neurologists
inside my brain like fantastik
voyage woke up in th middul
of th operation gave em a poetry
reading sure was fun they
put me out again sd i mustuv
known my way round drugs
cause they sure gave me a lot
well they got proof of th inter
cerebral bleed thing rescued
me from th shrinks who

still usd to sneak up th back
stairs to get at me but th nurses
usd to kick them back down
those neurologists and th nurses
in that ward sure were good
to me usd to lift th covrs off my
head which was liquifying or sum
thing my eyeballs turning to
mush ask me if there was
very much pain strong tendr
angel eyes iud say theres

so much pain don't worry we'll
bring yu anothr shot thank yu
iud moan and now i can even
write this tho th spastik fine
print in th elbow or wherever
it is is kinda strange but ium
sure lucky and grateful
fr certain that it was an intr
cerebral bleed

7 canduls

with th wind
blowing this
hard

there is
nothing
to hope

with this
bump on back
a my head

there is
nothing
to hope

th candul
is going
yu lit it

there is
nothing
to hope

th candul
yu lit it
is going

there is
nothing
to hope

shut out
th wind
flame

there is
nothing
to hope

a sea of
skulls in
th harbor

rainbow music

tonite ium with my sistr
        in th difficult subway
    undr th desert
and with my brothr in th fire tree

a way uv speaking with one n othr
   a way uv dreeming breathing. great toads
oak trees, straing to see. and th boats cum
   to take us all away

        we all uv us covrd
     with long flowing white hair

th accordion sings in our heart

        deep in th black pupil uv our
eye th star in th earth our arms in

    th watr and now th spirit sings
   my head deep between yr legs
      do yu like th band

   7 saturday nites tapestry uv wheat th yellow
flowrs in my belt
    th hills moving large nd endless ovr my tiny
head and what appears we nevr know

     our hair curls waving round our feet
   th soft lush grass undr us th release thru our
    spine

        no one wants to be alone
   thru th tight silences uv dark night th rain
is cum with th blessings uv th old ones.

    we heard my sistr nd brothr nd i what sum say
     yu cannot hear

may/71

thy holy name

      sum times trying to
see th way, sum times being part of
it

  th sun ovr th mountains ovr
th sea th lights around them all

all th seas turn to sand
to yu to shells rising

ring

in th centre a cushiond layer that
holds, and holds sum more,is th gentul
being. its turning out that way. trust
is reveald thru yr actions,as th
serpent catches up with saturn

th bright yellow flame in th centre,all tend
th warmth

yu are

NO ONE OWNS EARTH

     well they moved across th hill
looming large ya cud say, th soft
moon overhead will outwit us all,
th old ones hooted, th babes grunting,
well over th hill.

     th women's arms, soft as th moon,
making circles, like th trees down
into th valley, how to move
a whole peopul.

     we pray for our peopul, moving
together, to see this is how th Earth is,
Father, you let us walk on, live on,
teach us to grow together in Peace
on your Earth.

     Seeing Father how th Earth is as
Women, giving, giving, and making
wound, flood of her sorrow, we do
not know enuff, and giving, giving

     What is it, laughing how long th
sun rise, th hair of a whole peopul
sleeping under blankets, before fires, of
a whole peopul, on th hillside

     a long dream, third eyes flowing
within th wheat fields, endless
as th eye is, th eye of th peopul reaches
out to a new gathering

     cradled in the woman's arms, th
children stretch in th sun rays, for them
it is not a long dream, th world changed
as they slept, peed into Earth

    timber leaf time, before winter's
frost, slant limbs up thru th sunlight, how
far cud yu climb, well, i just saw a mountain
— and i aimd to get to th top of it, as Larry
sd, there is always a path for yr feet

   th moon, sailing over th water, bright orange
ovr th city, seen from th rising island, from
below, city dwelld eyes, pale yellow, th smog
so thick, th old Sun bldg., a monstrous invitation
thru th haze, on a clear day in th City.

hows that again, th moon, orange hunter's moon
seen from th island shining over th city, the same
moon pale yellow that night seen from th
city's street, th smog that heavy over th city

occur and see

yu stay in th city and soon yu go right down
david sd, as it seems yu reach out for yr
dream of sparrows, only they perch on wires
in th city, you can't make tracks on electricity, just south
of Clinton, B.C., there's a crimson lake, big one, shining,
alkaloids in th water, red liquid desert, closer
to th sparrows yu dream of

th mountain rain

comparisons are odious, but i sure dug
sleeping on top of a big pile of fresh baled hay,
musta been 15 feet up, more than on top of a pile
of pomes and th non-stop traffic, just south of Prince
George, best sleep i had in years i told Lenore,
when i came back from th Cariboo, beautiful
country

winter

th main road to Prince Rupert was blockd to traffic
in sum parts, had to take detours, that was along
th way to Rupert from Smithers, just past Terrace
i think it was too sum old roads with th doctor
whod driven non-stop from New York to Smithers on
dex in 50 hours, saw sum totem poles like hadn't
seen before, not shining with th paint sitting
just on top of th wood of th pole, but th color
growing out of th wood's color, not all filld in,
browns in rock at dusk, th figures knobbly, these
totem poles were not streamlined

islands

playing th stove rack with fork and spoon, magic
harp, i reached her, on th island, on top of one
of th mountains, there is a telephone wire relay
station, th calls between th islands, between
th islands and th cities, across water, what
they use to receive and send, suspended by
advanced technology, are like, *are* two big drums,
in th Bible it is said; there is nothing new
under th sun

let our arms grow to hold what we love

sunset

all ways, rivers to th sea of yr dreams, she
led me to a small clearing on top of that
mountain, just above th big drums, and all th
colors are true, rain forest ferns are such green

boulders on th road

at least they appeared there, as did th rustle up in th bush,
light gleaming down ahead of me, walking toward
th light, th bear rustle or whatever keeping pace,
light shining on th islands, a ride will cum by, to
return, at least that time they appeard, cock into cunt,
cock into cunt, hair sticking together love

writing on hard
bord

    sumbody's fingrs
   ar showin thru th
     sky

i aint skard

bralorne b.c. alright all th peopul thrown out

just dont get in my hair th man undr
th car gazing up at th crankshaft,
banging th axle again with his
monkywrench

                  i dont know wher
we'll live th hydro is going to cut
off th powr too   of course with th
mine's going, we'll all go sum

where, touching her head
as she walks back inside th
house that had 60 days
left, shed livd ther almost
that many years

                home is fragile
,histories drownin th verticul
present

        no one in th hotel,th gold mine spell
lookin down th cliff thousands a feet down,
them old verandahs straight up front,
th littul round tabuls yu feel all th old

times, th callous monymaking government
nd company town throwin it all out yu can
get an entire wellbuilt house with all th
new evn furniture in it fr 2 3 hundrid
dollars, course if yu buy it th company gonna make
yu get that home in th west off what they call ther
land ,within 30 days
                      th mine sz
                              all th controls gainst
ths business a moving forward, th loev in th rippd
off stream, o holy ethr in th hearts of

th peopul breathe, make it ther time ths
time, cost thousands a dollars to truck
any house offa that mountain to wher th land
is cheap enuff to put it on, amerikan summr homes hunting
lodgus land value too high for peopul who live here now
foreighn monopoly games choking us all, so th houses

burning

th homes on fire to clear th sold out land, sacrifice
for gods who dont care yet to take th time

                                                      th mountain,
raging rivr,creeks, magik grasslands until th peopul do

TH GREEN BRIDGE

do yu know how yu know
when yu lie asleep th birds
nest in yr dream. how th
green mountains peacefully
be. how th red forest is
lightning star. how yr thirsty
eye drinks th moon's wave. how
all ovr th world th grass
grows on yr belly. do yu know
how yu know

walkd across my life to get to yu,
thru 8 firing squads bravd th mists
of my own sumtimes doubting soul,
thru 3 veils of negation, but i blew
it cause one time before i hadint let
yu in, now there was no vacancy.

Yr loves will drive yu mad, give yu also
so much grace, touching yu with mercy.
yr love dusint go away, honor them, all of
th magical changes. they aint toys yu can
direct, they're othr animal spirits love
endlessly brings yu together all ovr th earth.

Yr life is now baby ovr and ovr again.
Try not to have to cry ovr so many
missd connections.let yrself love holy
being on this earth be there when yu are.
th grass of bright love grows up to yr
waist, th roots take yu into th sun.

Enjoy th opposition, yu saw
th ground fall in th air, all
th ways on fire, lakes & rivers
singd, yu are made of much
sea weed, why my hand is so heavy
on th pencil, why ium swimming in
th tea, undr th blue stars, th desert
is endless, dont do it if yr afraid.
th gods love yu too. i can smell my
sweat burning. in th chariot are
glistening lumps of bullshit. what
am i waiting for. we made our way thru
th palms, plungd on beyond th
doubting alligators, and it cudint
follow us, ovr th girders, we rose
with th floating surface.

We brot th bowl to th watrfall, th
spinning candles made th sign of
eternity. Outside th tent rising
to th sky all th flying sand.

mountain star

there is that a hundred times more
abiding. it is what we are moving
into, becum, of th place.

that th corners take us, bend round th
curve, th knot in th head unravel to
th music of our breathing

get it now, each time we dance undr th
moon and th cold

cats in heat all along melt th wall
of our undrstanding, moving trees

all our peopul and that includes yu call
out to us that we are all sorry

that it is sorry that th illusion
of need spins in th fire early

in our time we rage on with each othr
th hills bhind us around us we stir in

th night

fires in our head in our breast beat
that we dont know what it is

thru th rushing darkness th colors
move ovr evrything that we are

babies undr mountain and deer skin blanket
fierce also with wind wound & clear space

togethr on rays from th sun bring us into

th dawn

lookit th birds falling like leaves

out of th tree onto th seeds on th ground,
th tiger falls ovr, maybe hees asleep

taking th shells off eggs

it is there, nothing to call it
th land undr yr feet, th ice

itul get coldr,and then yul hear
th jack pine crack he sd. thanks

a lot for th ride. it got ya ther

th trees. snags falling rotting into
th earth. watr. yu dont even

think trees when yu walk undr
them. thru th moving way yu go

no names for, what is.

sparrows dream
of th endless sun, th rose in th forhead,
th sea cumming thru yr mouth, flowing
thru yr heart. children play with th
arrows, trees seem ageless deep in th
earth. there was a great light
around th floating mountain. we
came up high to th top for awhile.

dont worry yr hair

      dont worry yr eyes
     dont worry yr brain man th snow is
    cummin th bright burds flyin highr,th
sun is already all ovr yu,

     all th words all th mony all th unnecessary
    changes, a tree grows inside yu, let it and th bird
   red with blue circles,a white arrow on its side,sings
within yr breast, near yr spine, let its wings
   spread, yr arms

    each day probably sumhow yul get th watr

                            grow out to sum
   piece a land away from th bad business,th amerikan takeovr,to
  ward,into th earth yu cum from, have none of
th bargain with th tanks,th war heads

        each day th pebble is more stone,
  ium dreaming now of th place that will
soon have me, find me

             moving into th dark,it
is like going into a soft jewel. and being ther what at
first yu cud see nothing totally dark, only
  th feel of yr feet on th ground guides yu,

being ther, light apears here and ther,flashing,

yr head especially around th back breathes unfolds
opens like a flowr all around yu,

                 to th light

bare bones biography what els shudint i remembr

collage makr i do poetry readings hitch hikd bak n
forth cross canada bout 7 or 8 times flew coupul a
times done sum time inside too playd with th mandan
massacre fr a whil hav bin welfare recipient tutor
fcns buildr ditch diggr wintr works art gallry co-op
partnr th mandan ghetto help put out blewointmentpress
buks vancouvr startid with lance farrell nd martina clinton nd
othrs into vizual writing discovering *space* on a sheet
uv papr nd all yu can do with it nd th non gramatikul
line yeers uv poverty nd hard against th
correk line uv th ownrs — th faith to see how it can
be changes — once playd th student in goethe's faust
in halifax ths great halls bin lucky enuff to sit on
a few mountain tops wher i was born late 39 got out uv th
reserve air force thru brain damage was a teen age disc
jocky early paintr still am workd in garages very early
12 record store librarees staking buks sign paintr whn born i
weighed in at 12 lb 8 ozes pray that th world be mor open
as what is possibul that ther be less imperial isms ive seen th
sun rise and th amerikan empire set that th peopul share
diffrent undrstandings without one rule or sumwhun's
dominashun. one way is sure thru language sourse uv play
reverence pictures nd sounds. birds in th tree watr in th
earth whats in th sky sum times i dont know why. have
gone to a few dances at sum schools th professors didint
always believe it was me. ive nevr graduated from
anything. nu buks cummin out from blewointmentpress
by maxine gadd, gerry gilbert, bertrand lachance,
px belinski, bpNichol, ken west, nd others. th wheel nd
th drum uv the gestetener. thers a fire on th hill. love
nd th blessing to eat th coals in th hot snow.

                                          je.17/71

HOUSE OF ANANSI POETRY
(In Print)

The Circle Game, Margaret Atwood
The Dream Animal, Charles Wright
Airplane Dreams, Allen Ginsberg
The Army Does Not Go Away, David Knight
Year of the Quiet Sun, Ian Young
The Gangs of Kosmos, George Bowering
The Happy Hungry Man, George Jonas
Body, Robert Flanagan
The Collected Works of Billy the Kid, Michael Ondaatje
Sounding, eds. Jack Ludwig & Andy Wainwright
Power Politics, Margaret Atwood
Mindscapes, ed. Ann Wall
nobody owns th earth, bill bissett